A Kalmus Classic Edition

Wolfgang Amadeus

MOZART

OPERA OVERTURES

CONTENTS

FOR ONE PIANO/FOUR HANDS

K 02105

Overture to
DON JUAN

Secondo

WOLFGANG AMADEUS MOZART

Overture to
DON JUAN

Primo

WOLFGANG AMADEUS MOZART

Secondo

Primo

Secondo

Primo

Secondo

Primo

Overture to
THE MAGIC FLUTE

Secondo

WOLFGANG AMADEUS MOZART

Overture to
THE MAGIC FLUTE

Primo

WOLFGANG AMADEUS MOZART

Secondo

Primo

14

Secondo

Secondo

Primo

Secondo

Primo

Overture to
THE MARRIAGE OF FIGARO

Secondo

WOLFGANG AMADEUS MOZART

Overture to
THE MARRIAGE OF FIGARO

Primo

WOLFGANG AMADEUS MOZART

Secondo

Primo

24

Secondo

Secondo

Primo

Overture to
LA CLEMENZA DI TITO

Secondo

WOLFGANG AMADEUS MOZART

Overture to
LA CLEMENZA DI TITO

Primo

WOLFGANG AMADEUS MOZART

Allegro

Secondo

Primo

Secondo

Primo

Overture to
COSI FAN TUTTE

Secondo

WOLFGANG AMADEUS MOZART

Overture to
COSI FAN TUTTE

Primo

WOLFGANG AMADEUS MOZART

Secondo

Primo

Secondo

Secondo

Primo

Overture to
THE ABDUCTION FROM THE SERAGLIO

Secondo

WOLFGANG AMADEUS MOZART

Overture to
THE ABDUCTION FROM THE SERAGLIO

Primo

WOLFGANG AMADEUS MOZART

Secondo

46

Secondo

Primo

Secondo

Overture to
IDOMENEO

Secondo

WOLFGANG AMADEUS MOZART

Overture to
IDOMENEO

Primo

WOLFGANG AMADEUS MOZART

Allegro

Secondo

Primo

Overture to
L'IMPRESARIO

Secondo

Allegro assai

WOLFGANG AMADEUS MOZART

Overture to
L'IMPRESARIO

Allegro assai   **Primo**   WOLFGANG AMADEUS MOZART

Secondo

Primo

Secondo